PROBLEMS IN BUILDING CO

D0431623

WITHDRAWAL APPROVED
BY THE AA COUNCIL

PROBLEMS IN
BUILDING CONSTRUCTION

A Scientific Method Approach

J. TRILL, AIOB., ACSI., AMBIM.

Head of Department of Building, Croydon Technical College

J. T. BOWYER, Dip.Arch., FRIBA., FRSA., AIArb.

Lecturer, Department of Building, Croydon Technical College

ARCHITECTURAL PRESS · LONDON

ISBN 0 85139 552 X

First published 1972 by Architectural Press Ltd

© J. Trill and J. T. Bowyer 1972

Printed in England by H. E. Warne Ltd, London & St. Austell

Contents

Introduction

Much more emphasis is being given nowadays to involving students in the learning process through project work that extends and reinforces the knowledge gained by traditional teaching methods. Project work, however, is no soft option either for students or for the lecturer. To be effective, it has to be an organised and intellectually disciplined activity that puts the theories of the classroom to the test of real life situations.

Such is the object of this book. The authors have taken twenty actual case histories of building failure that in one respect or another illustrate points of construction with which students of building have come into contact during their first and second year of study. These are examined in a way which shows the principles of scientific reasoning at work in solving problems. Firstly a building failure is described through the eyes of a layman, usually a houseowner. In each case, the layman calls upon expert advice and at this second stage the student is asked to examine the answers which the expert has elicited from the layman to see what clues they offer about the cause of the trouble. From this point the case proceeds to a site investigation, the course of which reveals findings that cast further light on the trouble or confirm the investigator's original suspicions. At crucial points throughout each case study, questions are asked which test the student's knowledge and ability to relate formal syllabus material to practice. At the same time they provide clues to further lines of investigation in the case itself. At the conclusion the student is told the authors' own view of the cause and nature of the failure; and he is asked a series of further questions about the underlying technological and scientific basis of the problem and about possible remedies that might be effected.

It is obvious, of course, that at some stage in each case study the authors have had to let, at least partially, the cat out of the bag.

Because of the carefully structured nature of the material it will be seen that this does not in any way diminish the validity of the authors' approach; at the same time it should be said that to gain the maximum benefit from the text the reader is advised to answer each question as it comes up before proceeding to the next part of the investigation.

A tutors' guide to accompany PROBLEMS IN BUILDING CONSTRUCTION has been prepared. It provides detailed answers to the questions, explains the process of reasoning that is being followed and makes explicit the relationship of the various points that are being made to the syllabuses of the principal examinations in building. The students' text can, however, be used quite independently of the manual. In the solution of building problems many approaches may be valid and the authors would like to stress that they do not regard their own suggestions as more than one of several options. Indeed students and lecturers are encouraged to work out their own solutions, because the authors' principal objective is to show that the application of scientific method is at least as important as committing salient facts about construction science and technology to memory.

I. The case of the cracked corner

Situation

A client has called in with a problem—he had noticed a serious crack in one corner of the exterior wall of his brick-built house.

Verbal Investigation

In his office, the builder asked his client a number of preliminary questions to see if he could throw any further light on the problem.

(a) How old is the house?

(b) Has the crack got steadily worse, or did it develop suddenly?

(c) How long ago did it start?

(d) Is it near some external feature—e.g. a motorway—that could have caused the fault?

(e) Do other houses in the neighbourhood exhibit the same fault?

From the client's answers it emerged that the house was five years old, that the crack was first observed two years ago and had got steadily worse since. There was no immediately obvious cause and none of the surrounding houses had the same fault even though they had been constructed at the same time and were of the same design.

Q. 1. 1   Despite this apparent lack of evidence, the builder was able to deduce something from these answers. What was it?

Site Investigation: first stage

(a) On arriving at the site the builder began by looking at the crack. He noticed that it followed the horizontal and vertical brick joints in a diagonal line. It was wider at the corner of the building and extended through the full wall thickness.

(b) Next he investigated the environs of the building. He noted that a poplar tree was growing close by and that the lawn around this was crazed.

(c) A visual inspection showed a slight depression in the ground

9

around the tree which had been planted five years ago. The depression had become obvious in the last two or three years.

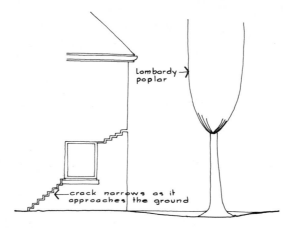

Starting out with these facts, the builder now asked himself some more questions, based on his knowledge of building construction.

Q. 1. 2 What types of failure are likely to cause a wall to crack through its full thickness?

Q. 1. 3 Why did the crack follow the horizontal and vertical joints?

Q. 1. 4 Why is the crack wider at the top than at the bottom?

Q. 1. 5 What could have caused the depression in the ground?

Q. 1. 6 What is likely to be causing the wall to crack?

Site Investigation: second stage

The initial investigation confirmed the builder's suspicion about the foundations supporting the cracked wall. His diagnosis, however, could have been made on the basis of a number of causes—it could have been the subsoil, it could have been the presence of the poplar tree, or it could have been a fault in the foundations—and so in order to investigate further a trench had to be dug alongside the cracked walls. From this the following facts emerged:

(a) The soil was examined and found to be heavy clay.

(b) The wall cracks extended down to a concrete strip foundation which was also found to be cracked. The portion of the foundation under the corner walls had settled and sloped down towards the corner.

10

(c) Roots from the tree were traced and found to be under the wall foundation.

(d) The top of the concrete foundation was located at a depth of 1.400 metres below ground level.

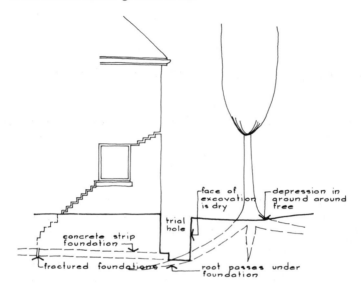

Conclusion

From this evidence the builder concluded that the cause of foundation failure was the poplar tree adjacent to the building. It was taking moisture from the soil, causing it to shrink and consolidate under the foundation load.

Q. 1. 7 What was the main evidence which pointed to his diagnosis?

Q. 1. 8 Under what circumstances can clay soils cause building failure?

Q. 1. 9 Why was the depth of the foundation measured?

Q. 1.10 How did the foundation settle?

Q. 1.11 Is there a possibility of further damage to the building? If so, of what kind and how can it be prevented?

Q. 1.12 Can the existing damage be repaired? If so how?

2. The case of the worried developer

Situation
The speculative developer of a housing estate called in a builder to investigate a complaint from a furious couple who had purchased a new two-storey house from him two years ago which had developed a serious and progressively deteriorating crack in the front wall.

Verbal Investigation
Over lunch before going on site the builder asked the developer some questions to see if there was any immediate and obvious cause for the situation he had described.

(a) Were there any signs of damage to other houses on the estate?

(b) Were there any signs of cracking in other parts of the building?

(c) Was there any possible external cause for the damage?—e.g. vibration from machinery?

The developer said that apart from the fact that the house in question seemed to be the only one affected and that a similar crack had appeared in the rear elevation, no clear ideas as to the cause of the trouble could be ascertained. Developer and client proceeded to the site.

Q. 2. 1   Although this answer was not very detailed what could the builder learn from it in investigating the cause?

Site Investigation: first stage
(a) The builder began by looking at the outside of the house. Making a visual examination of the crack, he noticed that the trouble had spread right up to the roof tile courses, where the vertical joints had opened up in line with the crack on the front elevation. This crack ran from the upper window to the top of the front door frame.

12

(b) The gable ends appeared to be out of plumb and were leaning out from the top.

(c) No surrounding buildings on view from the garden showed any signs of cracking.

(d) A closer examination of the wall crack revealed that the crack was wider at the top of the wall.

(e) The depth of the crack was probed and it appeared to extend the full thickness of the wall.

(f) Inside the house it was observed that the plastered surfaces of the outer walls were cracked vertically opposite the positions of the external cracks.

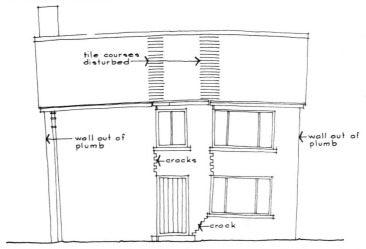

From his knowledge of building construction, the builder asked himself the following questions:

Q. 2. 2 What types of failure are liable to cause a severe crack down the centre of the building?

Q. 2. 3 What was the significance of the fact that the crack was also in evidence on the rear elevation?

Q. 2. 4 Why would the gable walls be out of plumb and leaning over from the top?

Q. 2. 5 Why have the cracks formed between door and window openings?

Q. 2. 6 What is the significance of the surrounding buildings being sound?

Q. 2. 7 What types of failure could cause this cracking?

Site Investigation: second stage

The initial investigations suggested that the cause of the trouble lay beneath the ground and so trenches were dug to examine the foundations and soil around the building. This inspection revealed:

(a) The walls were supported on concrete strip foundations situated 1.5 m below ground level which had cracked directly under each wall crack.

(b) The foundations at the centre of the building were in a different type of soil than those at the end. The soil at the centre was firm clay and at either end a mixture of a variety of soil types.

(c) Decaying metal drums were found in the soil at the ends of the building.

The builder was now convinced that the problem was associated with weaker or unreliable soil being present under either end of the foundations. He was just about to leave the site to arrange for the soil to be tested when an old local inhabitant asked him whether the house crack was one of the consequences of building on a rubbish tip.

Verbal Investigation: second stage

The builder asked him:

(a) What sort of tip was it?
(b) Where was it located?
(c) How long it had been in existence?
(d) How deep was it?

The old man said that the ground on which this house and a few surrounding ones had been built had been used, by the local inhabitants and some firms, as a tip for the past twenty-five years. Prior to this a number of small excavations, each about 4 metres deep, had been carried out and the clay carted away for use elsewhere. A few years before the site was developed all the holes had been filled.

The builder then asked him:

(a) If he could remember how many holes were dug.
(b) Whether there were any holes in the vicinity of the cracked house.
(c) How wide the holes were.
(d) If tipped material had been distributed in places other than the excavations.

The old man said that there were not many holes and they varied in size with the largest being approximately 15 m across. It was hard to remember whether there were holes near the house although he seemed to recall that a small hole lay either side of a track which went into the site somewhere near this house. Very little rubbish was tipped anywhere other than in the holes.

Q. 2. 8 What conclusions, if any, about the nature of the house failure could the builder glean from this conversation?

Conclusion

The builder concluded that the centre foundations had been built on good load-bearing soil, but that the ends were resting on unconsolidated soil to a depth of approximately 4.00 m below ground level. These findings were confirmed when a check at the record office showed that the building land had formerly been a rubbish tip.

Q. 2. 9 What remedial measures could be adopted?

Q. 2.10 What type of foundations are generally suitable for building on made up ground?

3. The case of the cut-price extension

Situation

To provide a self-contained living unit for his aged in-laws, a house owner sought and obtained planning permission to increase the length of his house by four metres. To save money, he had the drawings prepared by a friend engaged in building design work, and then employed various sub-contractors to carry out the work to his instructions.

Within two years of its completion, he asked a chartered surveyor to survey some serious wall cracks which had appeared at the junction of the new and old building on both wall elevations.

Verbal Investigation

The owner visited the surveyor's office and took with him the house drawings. When looking at the drawings, the surveyor asked some questions about the project and the construction of the building.

(a) How old was the original building?

(b) Had the owner noticed any cracks in the original building prior to the construction of the extension?

(c) Were there any other houses close at hand and had they cracked in any way?

(d) Were the basement walls in the old building cracked or showing any signs of failure?

(e) Were the foundations in the new building to the size and depth shown on the drawing?

(f) Was the ground quite firm under the foundations?

(g) Did the owner carry out regular inspections, and did the local authority inspector pay many calls?

(h) Could he think of any reason for the failure?

The owner thought the original building was fifty years old and, like surrounding properties close by, it showed no signs of cracks.

16

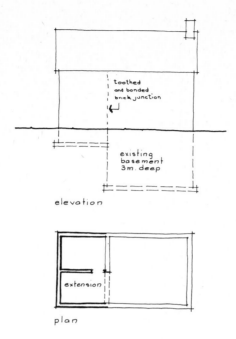

elevation

plan

Even the basement was in as good an order as the day it was built. As far as he could recall, the foundations were constructed to the drawings and the soil seemed quite firm. He was unable to think of any reason for the failure as he had kept a close watch on the construction and the local building inspector had also looked in from time to time.

Q. 3. 1 The surveyor was able to extract some important information from this visit which would narrow his field of investigation later on. What was it?

Site Investigation: first stage

(a) Following the meeting, the surveyor visited the house to carry out a more detailed inspection. On entering the garden, he had a full view of the front elevation and saw that the wall crack was quite noticeable and was located in the position described by his client. He also noticed that the roof tiling directly above this crack was disturbed.

17

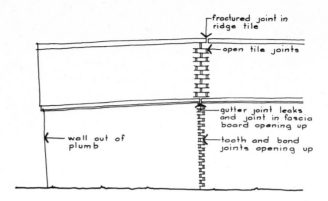

(b) He was then invited into the house, and following a general conversation concerning the scope of the survey, he took the opportunity to inspect the rooms. Vertical cracks in the wall plaster were noted which were approximately in alignment with the external wall cracks. All the ceilings in the new building were also cracked where they met the dividing wall between the new and old sections.

(c) There was no noticeable damage in the original building.

(d) Being aware of the disturbed roof tiles, he next inspected the loft or roof space and noted that daylight was penetrating at one of the ridge tile joints. He was unable to examine the other tiles because they were backed with roofing felt.

(e) Next, he went outside and established that the form of tile disturbance and cracking was the same on both elevations. He also noted that the end wall was out of plumb.

(f) A closer look at the wall revealed that the cracks were deep and not just confined to the brickwork joints.

(g) Finally, he looked at surrounding properties and found that they were similar in design and were in good structural condition but that a number of large brick boundary walls had cracked or were leaning over.

Using these observations, the surveyor asked himself the following questions:—

Q. 3. 2 What type of failure would cause a deep or complete crack in this wall?

Q. 3. 3 Why might the plaster crack at the junction of the dividing wall and new building ceilings?

Q. 3. 4 Could the disturbances in the roof tiles and light penetration at the ridge be associated with the wall failure? If so, what is the relationship?

Q. 3. 5 What type of failure would produce similar cracking on both elevations and cause the end wall to lean?

Q. 3. 6 Why are the surrounding buildings all in good structural condition when many of the boundary walls are not?

Q. 3. 7 What is the likely cause of the cracking?

Site Investigation: second stage

The surveyor had concluded, from his first investigations, that the failure could not be attributed to poor design or faulty construction. To investigate the cause further, the surveyor arranged for inspection holes to be excavated adjacent to the cracked wall sections and adjacent to the end wall. From this the following facts emerged:—

(a) The wall cracking extended right down to a concrete strip foundation.

(b) This foundation was in accordance with the size and depth below ground level agreed on the drawing (approved by the local authority). It was not joined to the old building and sloped down towards the end of the new building.

(c) The soil down to depth of two metres was loose and was primarily soft sandy clay.

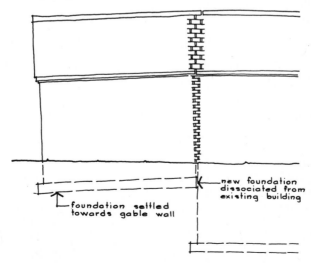

(d) The foundations of the old building were located in solid clay at a depth of approximately three metres below ground level.

Conclusion

From these and earlier findings, the surveyor concluded that the bearing capacity of the soil directly under the extension foundations was insufficient to prevent considerable settlement and contrary to his earlier conclusions this constituted a design failure.

Q. 3. 8   What was the main evidence supporting these conclusions?

Q. 3. 9   What are the primary factors influencing the bearing strength of soils?

Q. 3.10   What practical tests can be applied to identifying soil types?

Q. 3.11   What remedial measures and repairs should be undertaken?

4. The case of the isolated garage

Situation
Just before purchasing his first car, a young man became increasingly worried by the appearances of cracks in the floor and walls of his newly-built garage and asked a surveyor to visit his home to give advice.

Verbal Investigation
Over the telephone the surveyor asked the young man a number of questions to get a clearer picture of the problem confronting him.
(a) How long ago was the garage built?
(b) Who built it?
(c) Where exactly are the cracks located?
(d) When did he first notice them?
(e) Has the cracking got worse?
(f) Can he think of any reasons for the failure?
(g) Did the local building inspector visit during the construction period?

From the young man's answers, it was found that the garage was built six months ago by the young man and his father-in-law, who was a skilled bricklayer. He could not think of any definite reasons for the failures, and he had only noticed the cracks just recently because the very cold weather and snow had kept him out of the garden. There was a single crack in the floor slab parallel to one side wall and the crack in the brickwork ran along the other side wall. The building inspector only visited the site after it had been built.

Q. 4. 1 Was the surveyor able to deduce anything from these answers? What was it?

Site Investigation: first stage
(a) On arrival at the property, the surveyor noticed that the site

21

was on a sloping chalk site, and that to erect the garage it had been necessary to cut into the side of a chalk hill.

(b) Many other buildings had been erected by cutting into the hill, but as far as he could see they were uncracked and quite stable.

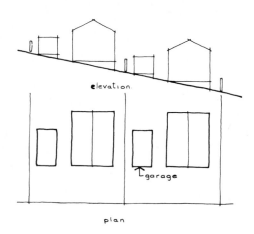

(c) He then looked at the crack in the outer wall and found that it ran horizontally along the brickwork joint at floor level and that the brickwork below this crack was not only bulging outwards but was obviously very damp.

(d) Moving round the outside of the building, he noticed that the other walls were uncracked and plumb but the ground adjacent to the other side wall was very wet.

(e) Finally, he examined the floor of the garage and found that the crack was located in the position which had previously been described over the telephone. It was quite wide and there were differences in floor level on either side of it.

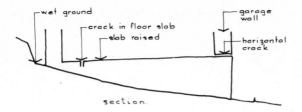

From these observations, the surveyor posed the following questions:—

Q. 4. 2 What type of failures can result from building on sloping sites?

Q. 4. 3 Is it likely that the cracks are the result of the garage being constructed on a sloping site?

Q. 4. 4 What could cause the brickwork to bulge beneath the horizontal crack?

Site Investigation: second stage
He then examined the drawings and noticed that there were differences in the wall foundation construction and that the slab rested directly on chalk and hardcore filling.

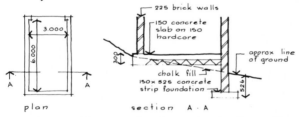

Q. 4. 5 What could cause the dampness in the wall, and could this, or its source, have led to the brickwork failure?

Q. 4. 6 Why should the other walls remain stable?

Q. 4. 7 Why would the ground adjacent to the opposite wall be very wet, and could this situation cause the building to fail?

Q. 4. 8 What type of floor failure could leave the slab at different levels on either side of the crack?

Q. 4. 9 What are the most likely causes of the cracking?

Site Investigation: third stage
The investigations convinced the surveyor of a need to examine the wall and floor foundations and the soil adjacent to them. Part of the

23

garage floor was taken up and small holes excavated down to the foundation on all walls. From this examination the following facts emerged:

(a) The wall foundations were built directly on to chalk and were located at the distances below ground level shown on the drawing. The chalk under the stable side wall was very damp.

(b) The floor slab was bearing directly on damp chalk filling mixed with concrete hardcore.

(c) The foundation to the front wall had not moved but the brickwork directly above it was overturning. Foundations to the other walls were firm and there was no failure of brickwork above them.

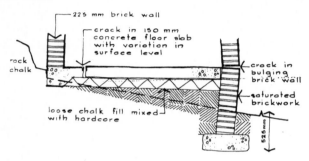

Conclusion

From these investigations, the surveyor concluded that the soil under the floor slab had frozen and caused it to uplift, crack, and so cause the brick wall to overturn.

Q. 4.10 What was the main evidence pointing to these conclusions?

Q. 4.11 Under what conditions could chalk freeze and cause the slab to lift?

Q. 4.12 How could these failures have been prevented or minimised?

5. The case of the observant house buyer

When looking over a house with an estate agent, the intending purchaser noticed that a brick wall bounding a garden terrace was not upright. He was very interested in making an offer for the property but was worried by the condition of the wall because it appeared to be supporting a considerable amount of earth beyond the terrace and looked dangerously unstable.

Verbal Investigation
He asked the estate agent if he thought the wall was likely to collapse and if the present owner had discussed the condition of the wall with him. The estate agent confirmed that when agreeing the selling price with his client consideration was given to the poor condition of the wall, but he was unable to say anything definite about the stability of the wall. The agent did say that he thought his client had the wall constructed about three years ago, but as he was now working overseas it would take some time to verify this and any other information required.

The prospective buyer had already arranged for a special survey of the property to be made by a professional surveyor, and so, following his visit to the property, he telephoned the surveyor and told him of his concern about the stability of the wall and the conversation he had held with the estate agent.

Q. 5. 1 Was the surveyor able to deduce anything from the information given over the telephone which would assist the investigation?

Site Investigation: first stage
(a) On entering the garden of the house, the surveyor noticed that the terrace had been cut into a steep sloping site and the leaning wall was supporting earth to a height of approximately one metre above ground level.

25

(b) He then looked at the gardens in surrounding properties and found that none of them had built terraces or had attempted to level the ground in any way.

(c) A general investigation of the wall and terrace revealed that the terrace paving slabs just in front of the wall were very water-logged and the brickwork at the bottom of the wall was damp.

(d) When he inspected the wall, he found that it was one brick thick and extended unbroken a distance of eighteen metres. Apart from the dampness, the walling materials looked to be in good condition.

(e) Finally, the earth at the back of the wall was very soft and wet.

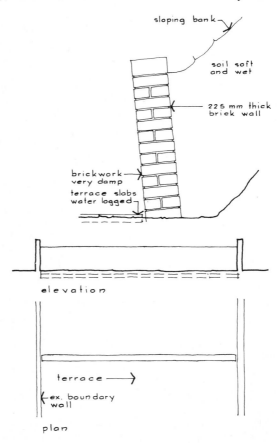

sloping bank

soil soft and wet

225 mm thick brick wall

brickwork very damp

terrace slabs water logged

elevation

terrace →

ex. boundary wall

plan

This prompted the surveyor to consider the following questions:

Q. 5. 2 In what ways can earth retaining walls fail?

Q. 5. 3 What is the significance of the damp conditions in the wall, the terrace paving, and in the retained earth?

Site Investigation: second stage

The surveyor was reasonably certain about the conditions primarily responsible for the wall failure. However, because he would be asked to recommend remedial measures and it was not yet possible to rule out failures in the structure below ground level, he decided to excavate inspection holes alongside the wall.

From the inspection holes, he ascertained the following information:—

(a) The brick retaining wall was in good structural condition and rested on a concrete strip foundation which sloped down towards the front of the wall.

(b) The site soil was clay which contained a number of sandy/clay water bearing seams. The filling behind the wall was saturated with water, very soft, and had a silty clay appearance. The filling extended down to the underside of the foundation.

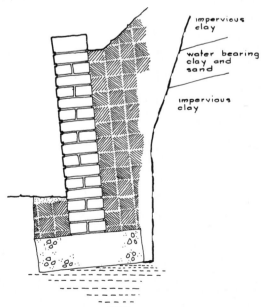

27

   (c)   The soil at the front of the wall and under the toe was saturated with water and very damp.

   This investigation posed the following questions:—

Q. 5. 4   Had the soil not been saturated, would the wall have been stable?

Q. 5. 5   Why had the soil become saturated?

Conclusion

The surveyor reported that the wall was unstable due to a build up of water behind it and, in the present saturated soil conditions was likely to collapse. He recommended that if the wall was still wanted remedial measures be adopted immediately.

Q. 5. 6   What was the main evidence to support the view that the wall was unstable and likely to collapse?

Q. 5. 7   If the wall was removed, how would the retained soil behave and what would its profile be like when it finally stopped moving?

Q. 5. 8   What improvements in the original construction could have been made to prevent or minimise this failure?

Q. 5. 9   What remedial measures can now be taken?

6. The case of the faulty junction

The owners of a firm with a building sited on the land of a large commercial undertaking expanded their business and sought and obtained permission from the land owners to extend their office. Shortly after occupying the new extension the firm asked the builder to visit the site to explain the reasons for wall and floor cracks which had appeared at the junction of the new and old buildings.

Verbal Investigation

Just before visiting the site the builder spoke to the foreman responsible for the work and asked him the following questions:—

(a) Were there any signs of cracking during the construction period and when the building was handed over to the client?

(b) Did the client's inspector visit the work regularly?

(c) Were any changes made to the original design by the client's architect or themselves?

(d) Did he have any problems in getting the labour force to provide the right quality work?

(e) Could he think of any reasons for the failure?

The foreman said he had not noticed any cracks and couldn't think of any reasons for them. The inspector visited the work at least twice a week and never complained about the standard of work or the labour force. Apart from changes in some floor and wall finishes the architect had kept to the original design and had provided very adequate drawings which helped considerably in ensuring that the building was properly constructed.

Q. 6. 1 Bearing in mind that neither the builder nor his foreman had yet seen the cracks the builder was able to start to narrow the field of enquiries from this conversation. What probable causes of failure would he be concentrating on?

29

The case of the faulty junction

Site Investigation: first stage

(a) On arriving at the site the builder and his foreman gained the impression that the new extension had developed a slight lean towards the old building.

(b) They then located the wall cracks and found that they were at the junctions of the old and new walls and ran vertically from ground to eaves level.

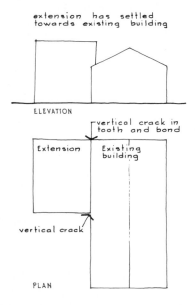

(c) A closer inspection of the cracks revealed that they were deep and had formed across bricks as well as along some vertical wall joints.

(d) They then looked at the ground floor rooms in the offices and found that cracking had occurred in the floor and ceiling on both sides of the wall dividing the new and old sections.

(e) Having completed their examination of the obvious damage around the dividing wall between the new and old sections, they extended their inspection to other parts of the offices. They found that apart from some ceiling cracks in the rooms adjacent to the dividing wall the other parts of the building showed no signs of damage.

30

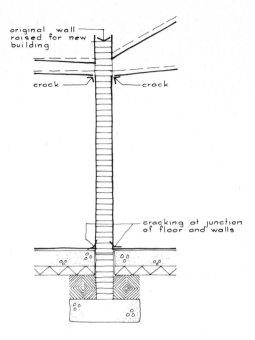

(f)   Finally, they looked at other buildings in the area and found
       no signs of similar damage but these were only single storey.

In a discussion following this visit the builder and his foreman
considered the following questions before drawing conclusions
about the failure.

Q. 6. 2   What type of failure would cause the extension to lean in
          towards the old building?

Q. 6. 3   Why were the cracks located at the junctions of the new
          and old walls?

Q. 6. 4   What could cause the floor to crack on either side of the
          dividing wall?

Site Investigation: second stage

The builder was now quite convinced that the dividing wall had
settled and furthermore that the failure had not been the result of
faulty workmanship on the part of his firm. Accompanied by a
structural engineer he arranged to meet the architect to discuss the
failure and look at the drawings.

At the meeting the builder absolved himself from blame and then left the structural engineer to discuss the design with the architect. In the discussions the engineer asked the architect:

(a) If he had undertaken extension work before and, if so, whether the designs were similar to this one.

(b) Whether the building had been constructed as shown on the drawings.

(c) If any investigation had been made of the old building foundations.

(d) If the adjoining wall and foundations had been strengthened.

The architect said that he had designed two single storey extensions which were similar in design but had not failed in any way. One of the extensions was built on an office situated just a few yards from the building in question. There was no evidence of foundation failure in this area in the past but nevertheless a trial hole was excavated to inspect existing foundations and soil conditions. As they considered the soil to be quite firm and found the profile of the existing foundation to be virtually the same as shown on the original drawings it was decided not to strengthen the existing foundations.

Following these discussions an examination of the drawings showed the engineer that the dividing wall was supporting one end of joists at first floor level and the concrete roof slab.

Q. 6. 5 From these discussions and the drawing inspection the engineer was convinced that he knew the reason for the wall failure. What was it?

Site Investigation: third stage

All parties were now convinced the reasons for the building failure lay in the foundations and to check this, holes were excavated alongside the wall cracks. The excavations revealed that:

(a) The soil was a fairly loose mixture of clay and sand.

(b) The existing concrete strip foundation had sheared directly under the cracks and when measured the strip was found to be 150 mm deep and 525 mm wide.

(c) The section of foundation under the dividing wall had settled below the level of the other foundations.

Conclusion

It was now agreed that the wall foundation had not been of sufficient size to prevent failure and settlement from the extra loading placed on it from the extension.

Q. 6. 6   What extra loads did the foundation have to sustain?

Q. 6. 7   What was the approximate percentage increase in the foundation loading?

Q. 6. 8   Would the foundation dimensions have seemed adequate for a two storey building and what guide lines do the Building Regulations provide in deciding the size of a foundation?

Q. 6. 9   How are the size of foundations for concentric wall loads decided by calculation?

Q. 6.10   What repairs can be undertaken in this situation?

7. The case of the mutinous tenants

Situation

When paying their rent at the local council offices the tenants of a recently constructed house complained of cracks in the floor tiles and threatened to withhold payment unless something was done about it.

Verbal Investigation

The rent officer told the tenant that he had no case for withholding rent but nevertheless if he would answer a few questions about the damage then arrangements could be made for an inspection to take place. The officer asked:

(a)   How long had the tenant been in the property?

(b)   Where were the cracks located?

(c)   When had he first noticed the cracks and had the situation deteriorated?

(d)   Had he any idea what might be causing them?

The tenant said he was the first occupier and had moved in three months ago. His wife had first noticed cracks in the floor tiles about two months ago but since then they had got worse and neither of them could think what had caused them. The cracks were close to the front wall in the lounge and dining rooms.

When their notes were passed to the maintenance supervisor for that estate, he was rather baffled and could only draw a few conclusions from them. He was particularly puzzled because the council had built several thousand houses of this type and with no failures of this type.

Q. 7. 1   What conclusions could be drawn?

Site Investigation: first stage

Arrangements were made for a convenient time for an inspection.

Before entering the house the supervisor saw water lying against the front wall. Without a more detailed inspection to determine the reason for this he entered the house and asked to see the cracks in the dining room and lounge floors. A close inspection of these ground floor rooms revealed:

(a) The cracks were quite deep, extending through the thermal plastic floor tiles and probably right through the concrete floor slab.

(b) The cracks were in a single line running parallel to and approximately 300 mm away from the external wall.

(c) The portion of flooring nearest the wall had sunk slightly below the level of the existing floor.

(d) Cracks had appeared in the plaster at the junction of the wall and ceiling.

Moving to other rooms it was observed that there were thinner floor cracks adjacent to all external walls. There was no signs of cracks in upper room timber floors but there were other plaster cracks at wall and ceiling junctions.

He next went outside and noted that the cause of the water lying against the building was the trough which was formed by the cracking and tilting of a concrete paving slab.

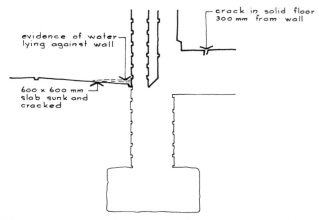

This inspection made the supervisor consider the following questions most seriously:

Q. 7. 2 What type of building failures could cause a concrete floor slab to break?

Q. 7. 3 Why would the cracks be located at a regular distance from either side of the outer walls?

Q. 7. 4 Why would the portion of slab nearest the external walls be at a lower level than the remainder?

Q. 7. 5 Could the cracking at the junction of the wall and ceiling be linked with this failure?

Q. 7. 6 Why would the cracks along the front wall be more pronounced than the others?

Q. 7. 7 Why would the garden paving lean in towards the wall?

Q. 7. 8 What is the likely cause of this failure?

Site Investigation: second stage

All the evidence suggested some form of wall settlement but the reasons for this were difficult to identify especially as this type of house had been constructed many times before and similar surrounding houses were in good condition. Therefore, the supervisor obtained agreement from the borough engineer to conduct an investigation of the foundations to the wall and slabs. Areas of the paving and floor slab were taken up and excavations were made down to the foundations which produced the following information:

(a) The concrete floor and paving slab near the wall were resting on a 150 mm layer of concrete hardcore bedded directly on to loose soil. In places this hardcore had sunk away from the underside of the floor slab.

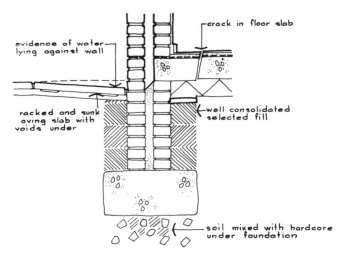

(b) The concrete strip foundation was the correct size and located at a depth of 1.2 m below ground level.

(c) Soil around the foundations was a mixture of loose clay and top soil.

(d) Soil had penetrated up through a thin layer of concrete hardcore under the wall foundation.

This investigation posed more questions about the nature of the failure and during a meeting between the supervisor and the borough engineer they asked themselves:

Q. 7. 9 How could this house fail when all similar types in this area and elsewhere had been satisfactory?

Q. 7.10 Why would soil under the slab and hardcore be loose and contain top soil?

Q. 7.11 What significance can be attached to the penetration of soil through the hardcore?

Conclusion

From the evidence the borough engineer concluded that the external walls and the adjacent floors and pavings had settled because unconsolidated site soil had been used as backfill. The wall foundations settled into the soft backfill and in so doing caused the fill around the wall to sink, creating a void under the slabs and paving. In sinking the walls pulled the edges of the slab and paving downwards, causing cracking.

Q. 7.12 What was the main evidence supporting the above diagnosis?

Q. 7.13 How could this situation have occurred?

Q. 7.14 How could it have been prevented?

Q. 7.15 What remedial measures can be taken?

8. The case of the harmless-looking damp patch

Situation

When redecorating a ground floor room in a council house prior to occupation by new tenants, the painter noticed a small patch of dampness on the inside of an external wall just above the skirting board. He thought it advisable to cease work on that wall and to show the dampness to his supervisor when he called later in the day.

Visual Inspection

When the supervisor arrived he looked at the patch, the surrounding walls, skirtings and floor boards and found dampness in the end of the floor boards adjacent to the skirting on that external wall.

He next went outside the building and noticed that the external wall was dry.

Verbal Investigation

The supervisor followed this brief inspection by asking the painter if he had observed any signs of dampness in the other rooms or in other properties on the estate.

The painter said that he was certain that no other dampness existed in the building and that he had seen no signs of dampness or similar wall patches in the one or two neighbouring properties that he had worked in during the past year.

Q. 8. 1   What conclusions about the nature of the problem can be drawn from this brief inspection and discussion with the painter?

From these preliminary investigations the supervisor decided to examine the construction drawings for the house and to look up previous maintenance records to see whether similar trouble had existed before.

Investigation of Documentary Information

The drawings and records revealed the following information about the property:

(a) It was built five years ago with twenty other similar houses in the same road.

(b) Only small repairs had been undertaken during the five years and none of them were concerned with walls, flooring or dampness.

(c) One of the other houses had dampness in an outside wall because of a faultily constructed damp proof course but the remainder had received only very minor repairs.

(d) The external walls were cavity brick construction.

(e) All ground floors were the traditional hollow timber type, comprising butted floor boards on timber joists fixed to timber sleeper wall plates.

(f) Ventilation through the wall was provided for the under floor area and the ground was covered by a concrete oversite slab on hardcore.

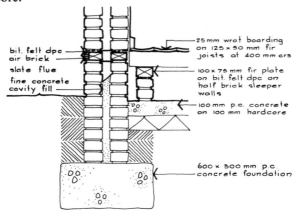

Following this document study the supervisor considered the following:

Q. 8. 2 By what routes could dampness enter the wall and flooring in this type of construction?

Q. 8. 3 What type of faults could develop within five years?

Q. 8. 4 Could this dampness be in any way related to the trouble experienced in the other house?

Q. 8. 5 What is the most likely trouble?

Before drawing any conclusions the supervisor thought it wise to carry out a more detailed inspection of the wall, flooring and underfloor construction.

Site Investigation

(a) The supervisor started the investigation by removing the timber skirting and floor boards adjacent to the wall. It was immediately apparent that whereas all the floor boards were damp, the skirting and wall were only damp in the vicinity of the observed damp patch.

(b) A closer examination of the wall dampness showed that it extended down to the damp proof course in a single patch. By raking out mortar joints it was possible to see that the mineral fibre damp proof course was not joined at a point below the patch.

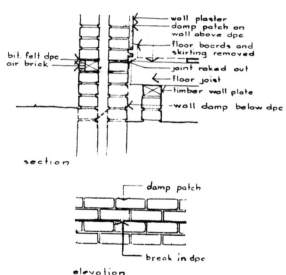

(c) Whilst looking at the patch the supervisor was aware of the damp musty atmosphere under the floor.

(d) He next went outside the house and raked out joints around the damp proof course in the outer wall skin at a point opposite the internal damp patch. From this inspection he was able to

40

see that there were no breaks in the damp proof course and to establish that the wall skin was perfectly dry.

(e) Coming inside again he now turned his attention to the damp-ness in the floor boards. Firstly the ends of the joists supporting the boards and the wall plate and brick sleeper wall underneath were very wet. The wall plate also had signs of rot. Looking more closely he noticed that the wall plate was bedded in mortar directly on to the sleeper wall. It was also wet throughout its length and not just adjacent to the damp wall patch.

(f) From an examination of the damp sleeper walls he noticed that the oversite concrete on which they rested was very damp and broken in places.

(g) Finally, the damp conditions under the floor prompted the surveyor to go around the outside of the building to locate and inspect the underfloor vents. There were a number of grills set in the wall between ground level and the damp proof course including one on the wall in question. When the supervisor went back into the house to locate and inspect the other side of the ventilator he found that the air bricks were only in the outer skin and did not go right through the cavity wall to ventilate the floor space.

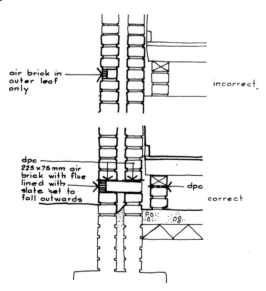

Conclusion

From this investigation the supervisor concluded that the sources of dampness for the floor and the wall were different. Both were due to rising dampness from the ground but the wall patch occurred because of a failure to lap the damp proof course in the inner skin of the cavity wall and the wet floor boards were caused by a failure to provide a damp course below the wall plate on the sleeper wall and lack of ventilation under the floor.

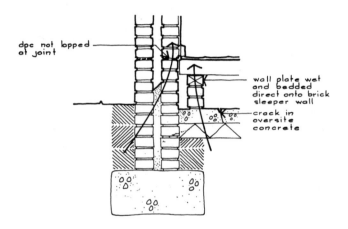

dpc not lapped at joint

wall plate wet and bedded direct onto brick sleeper wall

crack in oversite concrete

A check on other sleeper walls revealed that they had damp proof courses and the remedial work need only be restricted to one sleeper wall.

Q. 8. 6   What was the main evidence to support the theories that the dampness was rising from the ground and that there were two sources of penetration into the room?

Q. 8. 7   How does dampness rise in materials?

Q. 8. 8   What measures have to be taken to cure the dampness?

9. The case of the house that never dried out

The young owners of a new brick house, having noticed damp patches just above the skirting in their kitchen, were told by the builder that this was not unusual in a new property and could be attributed to drying out. They accepted this explanation but when after a further year the damp patches were even worse they sought the advice of a professional surveyor.

Verbal Investigation

They first met the surveyor at his office to explain their problem in more detail. After hearing a very general description of the situation and the explanation given by the builder he asked the couple some specific questions:

(a) How long has the house been built and when did they first observe the dampness?

(b) What type of external walls were they? Were they cavity type or brick throughout?

(c) Was the skirting damp?

(d) Were any other rooms damp?

(e) Had any of the neighbours experienced this trouble?

(f) Could they think of any reasons for the dampness?

They said that this was their first home and they moved in approximately two years ago on completion of the building work. The dampness was really noticeable after about nine months of occupation and when they asked their neighbours if they had similar trouble they said they had not. No other rooms were damp and they couldn't think why this one was although a friend said the rockery garden against that wall could be causing it. They were certain the wall was built of bricks but they confessed that they did not know the difference between one type of wall and another; the term cavity wall meant nothing to them. The skirting did not look damp.

Q. 9. 1 Could the surveyor get any useful information from their answers to help him diagnose the trouble? If so, what is it?

After this discussion the surveyor arranged to visit the house to undertake an inspection of the fault.

Site Investigation: first stage

(a)   Before entering the property the surveyor viewed the outside of the house and surrounding properties. He noticed that his client's house was the only one with a rockery against the wall and also that it was built up above the damp proof course. The brick stretcher bonding indicated that the walls were all cavity construction.

(b)   He then went inside his client's house and was shown the damp patches. They were just above the skirting on the external wall which had a rockery built against it. The patches were numerous and almost formed a continuous strip.

(c)   The skirting paint had bubbled and peeled in a number of places and the wood was obviously damp.

From this investigation the surveyor was able to decide how and where moisture was entering the brickwork. However, he decided to have a more detailed look at the construction.

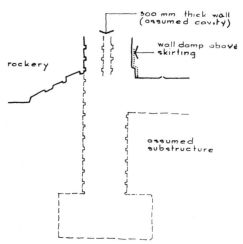

(d)   Finally he had part of the rockery garden removed which revealed very damp brickwork and a vertical open brick joint which is normally used to drain a cavity of any collected water.

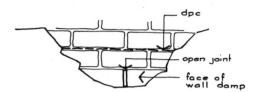

(e)   The surveyor decided to check the open joint to see whether it was clean and able to drain the cavity. He found that the probe would only just penetrate the depth of the outer wall skin and on checking other open joints around the building he found that a few of them would only allow penetration to a similar depth.

   The surveyor considered his findings before proceeding further and asked himself the following questions:

Q. 9. 2   Why would the probe only penetrate the depth of the outer brick skin?

Q. 9. 3   Could this blockage in the joints have led to dampness penetrating to the inside of the building?

Q. 9. 4   How is dampness entering the kitchen wall?

Site Investigation: second stage

In view of the difficulty of finding out if the wall was effective in stopping the penetration of dampness the surveyor decided to remove some of the outer wall skin around the rockery area and in places where open brick joints were found to be blocked.

   These investigations revealed that the concrete cavity wall filling

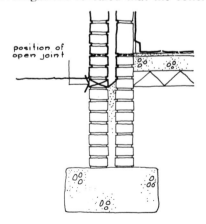

had been placed above the level of the damp proof course although in a few places the filling was below the damp course.

Dampness had penetrated through the cavity filling and into the inner skin above the damp proof course in the area of the rockery only. Everywere else the cavity filling was dry.

Conclusion

These final investigations confirmed the surveyor's opinion that moisture had come from the rockery and showed him that the vehicle for its transfer to the inner skin had been the concrete cavity filling built up above the damp proof course level.

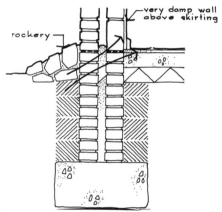

Q. 9. 5　What were the really important clues in arriving at this conclusion?

Q. 9. 6　What guidance do the Building Regulations give in the positioning of damp proof courses at ground floor level?

Q. 9. 7　What remedies can be adopted in this situation?

10. The case of the suspect married quarters

Situation

Following the January posting of a soldier and his family to an overseas military establishment arrangements were made for an inspection to be made of his married quarters so that any necessary repairs and maintenance work could be undertaken before a new family moved in. When looking over the house the inspector for the maintenance organisation was surprised to find a few small damp patches on the external wall in the dining room. As the house was only eighteen months old his first reaction was to suspect that some liquid had been spilled or sprayed on to the wall.

Verbal Investigation

The inspector drew the couple's attention to the marks and asked them a number of questions to establish the blame for the damage:

(a) How long had the marks been there?

(b) What had they spilled on the wall?

(c) Why hadn't they reported the marks until this stage?

The soldier said that they hadn't spilled anything on the walls and had only just noticed the marks in the past two or three months. His wife said she thought she saw signs of damp patches last spring when cleaning the walls down but as these disappeared in the summer she assumed that they had occurred because the house was drying out.

Not being entirely satisfied with these answers, the inspector asked:

(d) When had they taken occupation of the quarter?

(e) Had the builders looked over the property at the end of the maintenance period?

(f) Had any of the neighbours spoken of similar problems?

The couple said they were the first occupants and moved into the quarter in May eighteen months ago. They couldn't remember an inspection by the builder and their friends in the other houses had not spoken of similar trouble.

Q.10. 1 Although not absolutely satisfied with the replies to his questions the inspector was able to draw some conclusions from them. What were they?

Site Investigation: first stage

(a) The inspector took a closer look at the offending wall surface and found other fainter damp patches.

(b) Standing back to observe the wall as a whole he noticed the patches appeared to be fairly circular in shape and were spaced at regular intervals along and down the wall.

Measurements of the patch spacing showed that they were approximately 900 mm apart along the wall and at 450 mm intervals vertically.

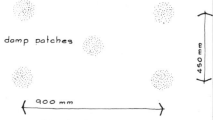

(c) He then went outside the house to look at the external surface of the wall and from the bonding established that the wall was of cavity construction. The wall was facing the south west and looked in very good condition except for a few hairline cracks between the mortar joints and the bricks.

These investigations prompted the inspector to ask himself some further questions:

Q.10. 2 Why would the patches be circular and at such intervals?

Q.10. 3 What type of dampness penetration could be associated with a cavity wall?

Q.10. 4 Is there any significance in the geographical location of this wall?

Q.10. 5 Could the hairline cracks in the joints be associated with the patches of dampness?

Q.10. 6 What is the most likely cause of the dampness?

On returning to his office the inspector verified the age and construction of the house and was so convinced that water was passing through the wall from the outside that he decided to inspect the wall cavity. Bricks were removed from the outer skin of the wall and it was seen that:

(a) Brick rubble and mortar droppings were lodged on a number of cavity wall ties.

(b) The waste material on the ties was in many cases quite damp.

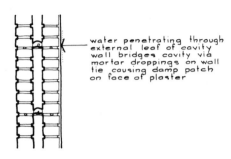

water penetrating through external leaf of cavity wall bridges cavity via mortar droppings on wall tie causing damp patch on face of plaster

Conclusion

From this evidence the inspector prepared a report which said that the damp patches were caused by rainwater passing through the external wall.

Q.10. 7 What was the main evidence for this conclusion?

Q.10. 8 How could this type of construction failure arise and how could it be prevented?

Q.10. 9 How can the fault be rectified?

11. The case of the damp prestige offices

Situation

A small firm employed on public relations work rented new luxury offices on the upper floor of an office development. The firm met many very important people and so had the offices decorated and furnished tastefully. After one year of occupation they were very disturbed to find damp patches appearing at the junction of the external wall and ceiling and promptly asked the developer to look into the matter and correct it forthwith. The developer who was very committed with new work asked an established local builder to visit the offices and make any necessary repairs.

Verbal and Preliminary Site Investigation

When the builder arrived he was met by the office manager who explained the importance of the offices to the firm and asked if any repairs could be speedily undertaken. The builder said he would do his best to cure the trouble quickly but the time this would take would obviously depend on the nature of the fault.

They then went to look at the dampness and the builder noticed that there were two patches at the junction of the external wall and ceiling which were approximately 3 m apart. In both cases the patches had developed in the wall and ceiling and there were signs that the wall plaster was bulging.

The builder, who had not seen any drawings of the building, then asked the manager a number of questions:

(a)   Had the dampness developed gradually and when was it first noticed?

(b)   What part of the building lay directly above this office?

(c)   Had any of the other tenants complained about dampness?

(d)   Could he think of any reason for the dampness?

The office manager said that the damp patches had gradually got

50

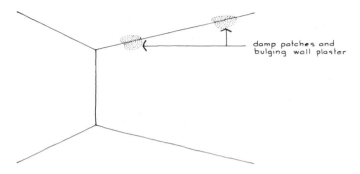

damp patches and
bulging wall plaster

larger from the time they were first noticed six months ago. Just
prior to this there had been a rather prolonged period of rain
and some people thought that the flat roof above the office was leaking; others suggested that water was getting through the coping
stones on the parapet wall which lay directly above the office external
wall. Personally he couldn't think what was causing the trouble and
certainly this office was the only one affected in the whole building.

Q.11. 1 So far this visit and conversation was useful to the builder
in making a preliminary assessment of the cause of the
trouble. What could he learn?

Site Investigation: second stage

(a) The builder then went on to the flat roof to continue his investigation and found that the roof slab was covered by mastic
asphalte and surrounded on all sides by a brick parapet wall
which was capped by concrete coping stones. The roof drainage
was via gulley points placed at the centre of the building so that
the roof sloped away from the walls towards the centre.

(b) The roof falls were quite generous and there were no signs of
water lying on the surface or faults in the asphalte covering.

(c) On inspecting the junction between the parapet wall and the
roof it was noted that the asphalte upstand had bulged away
from the wall at a position which would be approximately
above one of the damp patches. A closer look at this bulge
revealed that the upstand had not been tucked back into the
brick wall joint in one place.

(d) The inner face of the parapet wall located above the damp wall
faced north and was by comparison with the other parapet

51

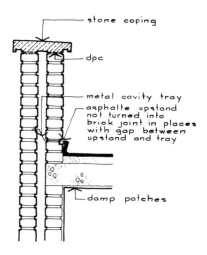

walls quite damp. The wall surface behind the detached up-stand felt extremely damp.

(e) By peering over the parapet wall the builder was able to see that the outer faces of the wall were quite dry and there were no signs of persistent dampness. The brickwork and jointing were in good order.

(f) He next inspected the coping stones. A number of the vertical joints between stones, at various points around the wall, had hairline cracks and a few of the drips on the underside of the stones were bridged and had caused water to discharge down the face of the wall. The damp proof course under the stones appeared to be correctly constructed and complete.

The builder now took time to consider the following questions:

Q.11. 2 Could water collecting on the roof cause the trouble?

Q.11. 3 How could the break in the asphalte upstand tuck-in be responsible for the dampness reaching the inside of the building?

Q.11. 4 Why should the inner face of the parapet wall be damp?

Q.11. 5 Could the failures or faults in the coping stones have contributed to the dampness?

Q.11. 6 What has caused the dampness?

The builder was quite certain the rain had got into the wall behind the asphalte upstand and because of difficulties in evaporating again had travelled down the wall to reappear as a damp patch in the

52

office. However, this did not account for the other patch as he considered it unlikely that dampness would travel along the wall or roof and reappear at just one point some 3 m away. He therefore decided to undertake a closer examination in the roof area vertically above the damp patch and sent for one of his men to assist him.

Site Investigation: third stage
(a) By taking measurements the builder found the section of the parapet wall directly above the damp patch. He was immediately struck by the dampness of the wall surface and the presence of a blockage in the coping stone drip.

(b) The asphalte upstand was firmly tucked into the brickwork and there were no signs of faults in the roof covering which would allow water to enter the structure.

(c) The builder decided that an investigation of the brickwork behind the upstand should be made. He had the upstand cut partly away from the wall and the joint around the damp proof course raked out. The inspection revealed that the brickwork behind the upstand was very damp and wall damp proof course was cracked.

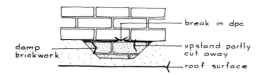

Conclusion
The builder concluded that the damp patches had arisen because water had got into the brickwork below and behind the damp proofing through faults in the damp proofing construction.

Q.11. 7 What was the main evidence for this conclusion?

Q.11. 8 How can these faults be remedied?

12. The case of the suspicious coincidence

Situation

When taking a morning cup of tea with a neighbour in her adjacent flat, a woman noticed similar damp patches on the surface of an external wall to the ones she had seen in her own flat. She discussed the problem with her neighbour who said that the patches had appeared almost three years ago when she and her husband took possession of the flat in February. By the spring there was hardly any sign of them and they considered that the building was just drying out. Last year the patches reappeared in the winter and faded a little in the summer only to return again this winter. These events were almost identical in both flats so the women, who were fed up with the unsightly stained walls, decided to have a word with the janitor.

Verbal Investigation

Having heard what they had to say, the janitor asked them:

(a)   Were there damp patches on the other walls in the flats?

(b)   Where were the patches located?

(c)   Had they any idea what was causing them?

The women said all the patches were on the external wall in both the dining and kitchen areas. In the dining area they were located at the junction of the wall and ceiling. There were also various patches on the wall and around the window opening. There was some dampness around the window opening in the kitchen area.

One woman wondered whether the driving rain on the outside of the wall was coming through, especially as they were the top flats in a high block and the wall was very exposed to the weather. The other woman said her husband thought the flat roof might be leaking because they were always troublesome and often leaked.

The janitor then 'phoned the council surveyor's department and related all the information given so far including the views on the cause of the dampness.

The surveyor asked the janitor to make an appointment for a visit to the flats on the following day and to ask the women whether the dampness had got progressively worse since they had first begun to notice it. They confirmed that the patches had got larger and the dampness remained longer than at first.

Q.12. 1 What, if any, clues to the cause and nature of the dampness could the surveyor glean from this telephone conversation?

Examination of Records

Following this conversation the surveyor could not help but reflect on different positions at which the patches occurred and so he sent for the drawings and specifications to search for further clues. His examination revealed the following information:

(a) The building was five storeys high and the flats in question were located on the top storey.

(b) The rooms in question were described as kitchen/diner which meant a 7 m × 4 m room divided into a cooking and eating area by the provision of a dividing unit comprising a working top with cupboards under and some high level cupboards.

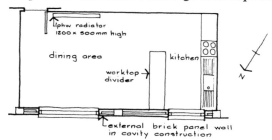

(c) The external wall to the rooms was brick cavity panel construction in a reinforced concrete frame.

(d) The damp wall was exposed to north west winds.

(e) The roof was flat, built in reinforced concrete covered with roofing felt.

Q.12. 2 What, if any, extra clues to the cause of the dampness come from examination of these documents?

Site Investigation: first stage

The day on which the surveyor visited the flats was cold and damp

55

and on entering the dining/kitchen room he immediately noticed the dampness at the wall and ceiling junction and around the window opening. He also saw that the other wall patches were all located half way along the 7 m wall around the position where a concrete column should be located.

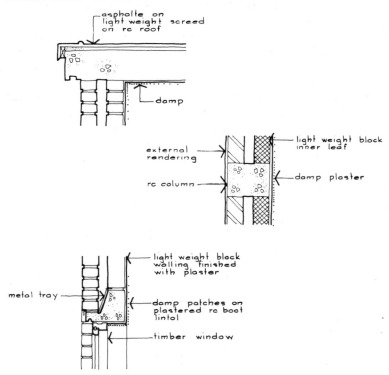

The occupier of the first flat apologised for coldness of the room and said that she had only just lit the oil stove. She added that the room often felt very damp and cold during the morning and she found the hot water radiator quite inadequate for heating this room.

A closer examination of the dampness showed that:

(a) All the patches were streaked at their lower edges.

(b) The wall paper on the dining area wall was bleached in the areas of the dampness.

On visiting the second flat the woman apologised for the absence of heating in the room. She said that the radiators had not been turned on as she was doing the weekly washing and the steam from the washing machine and sink would make her feel uncomfortably warm if the heating was on as well. The woman also mentioned the need to supplement the central heating with an oil stove in very cold weather. The room was certainly very cold in the dining area and the surveyor was quite aware that both of these women may have agreed among themselves to emphasise the poor heating standards in their rooms.

An inspection of the patches revealed that they were located in the same positions as in the other flat and were similar in size and shape. The patches were extremely damp.

The condition of these rooms now posed some important questions as follows:

Q.12. 3 Could the cold conditions in the flats be in any way responsible for the damp patches?

Q.12. 4 Has the location of the patches anything to do with the dampness?

Q.12. 5 Can anything be learned about the cause of the dampness from the shape of the patches and the bleached condition of the wall paper?

Q.12. 6 Why might the wall patches in the second flat be extremely damp by comparison with those in the first flat visited?

Q.12. 7 What is the most likely cause of the dampness?

The surveyor was almost certain about what was causing the dampness but before drawing a final conclusion he decided to examine the roof and wall.

(a) There was an easy access on to the roof via the tank room and the surveyor found that the roof felt was torn close to the outer wall in one place and the under screed was exposed and damp. The wall was not excessively damp under the position where the torn felt had been located.

(b) By firstly viewing the outer brickwork from the flat windows and then viewing it through binoculars from the ground, the surveyor considered it to be in very good condition with no signs of permanent or excessive dampness or weakened joints.

Conclusion

The surveyor now felt confident enough to conclude that the dampness was due only to condensation.

Q.12. 8 What was the main evidence supporting this conclusion?

Q.12. 9 Why and how does condensation occur?

Q.12.10 What are the most common causes of condensation in domestic buildings?

Q.12.11 How can the risk of surface condensation be minimised?

13. The case of the reappearing dampness

Situation
A young married couple approached a surveyor to investigate the cause of dampness at the junction of the party and front wall in both the upper and ground floor rooms of their semi-detached house.

Verbal Investigation
The surveyor received their letter and by arrangement asked them to visit his office. On arriving they told the surveyor that the patches were present when they first bought the house three years ago but they were then assured by the owner that the trouble had been cured and the walls were now drying out. After a few months the patches appeared to fade so they went ahead with decorating the room including wall papering. Alas, within the year the dampness had reappeared and had been getting worse ever since.

The surveyor now took the lead by asking a number of questions:
(a) How old is the building?
(b) Is the dampness right down the wall junction or in patches?
(c) Is the dampness more noticeable in some places and does it extend far along the party wall?
(d) Did the previous owner tell them what had caused it before?
(e) Had the adjoining owners noticed any dampness at the wall junction?
(f) When did they move into the house?

The couple said the house had been built in 1932 and they had moved in in the late spring of 1968. At the time of purchase they had tried to reduce the house price on the basis of having to cure the dampness but they were assured by the owner the trouble had arisen because of a leaking valley gutter located directly above the party wall. The adjoining owners had confirmed that the repair had taken place and had claimed that their walls had been dry ever since. Were reluctant to discuss the matter further.

Dampness had spread along the party wall and in particular was noticeable near the ceiling in both rooms and also just above the skirting level in the lounge.

The surveyor then asked the owner to describe the position of the valley gutter and its outlet to discharge the water.

A sketch was then drawn by the owner to answer his question.

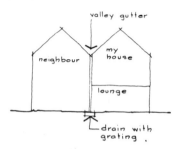

Q.13. 1 The surveyor found this meeting particularly useful in formulating possible causes of the trouble. What did he learn to help him?

Site Investigation: first stage

(a) Before entering the house the surveyor noticed that there were a number of other semi-detached houses of a similar style and that one or two of these properties had had new down piping fitted from the valley gutter. In contrast the brick wall had been rendered on only one property.

(b) He then went into the house and was shown the damp patches. They were positioned where the owners had described and were certainly very noticeable and wet-looking close to the ceilings and the ground floor skirting.

(c) The surveyor tapped the wall with his knuckles around the damp patches and found that the wall plaster near the ceilings sounded hollow.

(d) Paint work on the skirting was observed to be forming into bubbles and on bursting them moisture came out. The skirting and adjacent floor boards felt very wet.

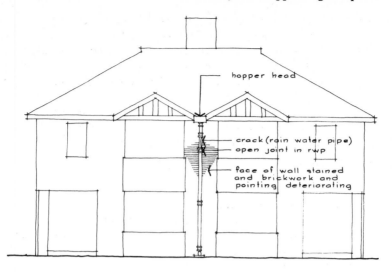

Following this inspection the surveyor considered the following questions:

Q.13. 2 Was there any significance in the fitting of new down piping and the rendered walls observed in other properties?

Q.13. 3 Why would the plaster sound hollow?

Q.13. 4 Why might the dampness be worse in certain places?

Q.13. 5 What type of dampness penetration would make skirting and floor boards damp?

Q.13. 6 What is causing the trouble?

The surveyor now felt certain that water was penetrating the external wall at a number of points and decided to examine the outside wall.

Site Investigation: second stage

(a) Going outside the surveyor immediately noticed the damp condition of the brickwork behind and around the down pipe and also that the bricks had spalled at the surface.

(b) By scratching the mortar wall joints with a penknife he found them to be soft to quite a depth.

(c) There was also extensive rainwater staining and brick-spalling at the down pipe joints which were located near the gutter, midway down the wall and at a shoe which directed water into a dished gully.

61

(d)   The ground around the gully was extremely wet.

(e)   The brick wall was solid, one brick thick.

Further important questions arose from the external inspection:

Q.13. 7   What could cause the brickwork behind the downpipe to be so damp and why should it be so pronounced at pipe joints?

Q.13. 8   Under what conditions would brickwork spall?

Q.13. 9   Why would the jointing mortar be so soft?

Q.13.10   Why is the ground so wet around the gully?

Q.13.11   How is the dampness entering the wall?

Conclusion

The surveyor was convinced that water was coming out of small corrosion pits in the pipes on to the wall and had over a number of years saturated it. The damage had been extended by frost action which had caused the brickwork to spall and wall joints to crumble; this in turn made damp penetration easier. The dampness around the gully was due to water running down the wall on the ground.

Q.13.12   What was the main evidence for this conclusion?

Q.13.13   What remedial measures can be undertaken?

14. The further case of reappearing dampness

Situation

Following the surveyor's advice, the young couple, referred to in Case 13, arranged for the downpipe to be renewed, some bricks to be replaced, and the wall re-pointed. After two years all signs of dampness had gone except at the ground floor level where it remained and was judged to have got a little worse. The couple wrote to the surveyor and asked for a further opinion.

Verbal Investigation

The surveyor was surprised by the contents of their letter and telephoned the couple to clarify the position. He asked them:

(a) Was the outside face of the wall damp?

(b) Was the ground around the gully very wet?

(c) Could they think of any reasons for the continuing dampness?

In reply, the couple said the ground was very wet and the wall was damp to a height of approximately 300 mm above ground level. They did wonder if water was splashing on to the wall from the gully during heavy rainfall—on one occasion they observed that the gully had overflowed during a heavy downpour of rain.

The surveyor found this conversation useful in forming some ideas about the nature of the problem and decided to visit the house with an assistant to make a closer inspection of the area.

Q.14. 1 What leads has this conversation given him?

Site Investigation: first stage

(a) On arriving at the house, the surveyor drew his assistant's attention to the fact that the wall faced north and the garden was rather shaded from sunshine by trees and bushes and shrubs.

(b) They then made their way to the gully and noted that new plastic piping had been fitted and that the repaired wall, at eye level and above, looked dry and in good condition.

(c) Pushing aside the privet hedge which divided the semi-detached houses, they noticed that the ground was very wet and that the gully had been raised by two courses of brickwork from its original height prior to the repairs.

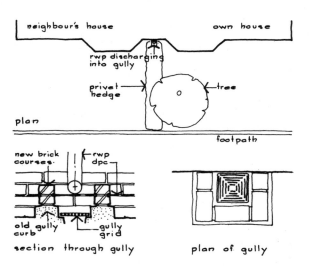

(d) A closer inspection revealed that the wall was quite damp to a height of four courses of brickwork above the top of the gully.

In a discussion that followed, the surveyor and his assistant raised the following points:

Q.14. 2 Could the northern and shaded aspect of the wall have any influence on the wall remaining damp? If so, what influence?

Q.14. 3 Why had the gully been raised, and had this been done to prevent further trouble?

Q.14. 4 How was water getting into the wall?

Verbal Investigation: second stage

(a) The surveyor did not like the construction of the gully, particularly as the new surround touched the house wall above the damp–proof course and could, therefore, transfer dampness into it. However, in view of the extent of the dampness, the

64

surveyor and his assistant were not convinced that this faulty construction could be a major contributor.

(b) They then called on the owners and asked them why the gully had been constructed. In reply, the owners said there were two reasons given by the builders, which were:

(i) The plastic pipe discharged too far above the gully and might have caused splashing of the wall and ground.

(ii) It would prevent overflow on to the ground during heavy rain.

The owners added that the flooding or overflowing had stopped as far as they knew.

Q.14. 5 These conversations revealed a number of important clues to the cause of the dampness. What were they?

Site Investigation: second stage

(a) The surveyor and his assistant were quite convinced that water was collecting in the gully and entering the brickwork above the damp-proof course and so decided to test it.

(b) They carried out this test by tipping water into the gully. This experiment revealed that it was quite easy to fill the gully to the point of overflowing and that the water was very slow in draining away.

Q.14. 6 This raised the following question. Why might the gully not drain easily?

Site Investigation: third stage

(a) The surveyor being convinced that a blockage in either the gully pit or the underground drainage run was causing water to build up in the gully, advised the couple to employ a builder to inspect and repair the drain. This advice was accepted and the builder arrived to carry out the work.

(b) First of all the builder cut back some of the privet hedge and dug down to expose the pipes. He found that the pipes were not encased or jointed and were choked with roots from the privet hedge.

Conclusion

On being informed of the builder's findings, the surveyor concluded that water had built up in the gully to a height above the damp-proof course and had entered and penetrated the house wall.

Q.14. 7 What was the main evidence for this conclusion?

Q.14. 8 Why would the roots of the privet enter the pipes in such density?

Q.14. 9 What remedial measures should be undertaken?

15. The case of the disfiguring white substance

A local authority had a new community centre built which was two storeys high and constructed in brick. The building was in a prominent position in the town and was used when entertaining local and visiting dignitaries. At a local authority works committee meeting, the borough engineer was asked by a local councillor why the parapet wall of the community centre looked so unsightly.

Verbal Investigation
The borough engineer was quite unprepared for this remark and had never noticed any faults. So to gain time to think and to get insight into the problem, the surveyor asked the councillor if he was referring to the design of the wall which had been given careful consideration at the Town and Country Planning approval stage.

To this the councillor said that he was quite pleased with the design but was merely referring to unsightly white stains running down the brickwork and a general white powdery look on the face of the wall.

The engineer, knowing the problems that can arise if statements made in the committee are proved to be wrong, was cautious in his reply. He said that many stains in brickwork were not serious and that he would look into the matter the next day and report back within the week.

From the councillor's descriptions, the engineer was quite certain what the staining was but not certain what was causing it.
Q.15. 1 What is the staining likely to be?

Site Investigation: first stage
(a) It was raining the next morning but, as promised, the engineer with his building inspector visited the municipal building.
(b) On arriving, they viewed the wall from the street and could

clearly see dirty white stains below the coping stones at a number of places along the wall.

(c) By viewing the stains through binoculars, it was possible to see water running from the under edge of the copings down the stained brickwork.

(d) There was no sign of the white powdery surface on the wall.

Both the engineer and his inspector were agreed that a closer examination was needed of the coping stones and the stains. However, before taking this look, they had arrived at a possible conclusion by considering these questions:

Q.15. 2 What type of staining could occur from water running off the coping stones on to the wall?

Q.15. 3 Why might water be running off the stones on to the wall?

Site Investigation: second stage

(a) The sun was shining the next day and after lunch the engineer and inspector returned to the building for a detailed inspection of the parapet wall and stains.

(b) On arriving outside the building, they noticed that the parapet wall brickwork had a white powdery look.

(c) Moving up on to the flat roof, they immediately noticed that the inner side of the parapet wall was similarly stained but the bricks were only slightly covered by the white powdery substance and this was in a few patches near the coping stones.

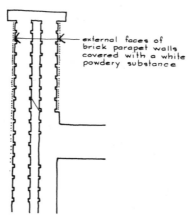

external faces of brick parapet walls covered with a white powdery substance

They next took a closer look at the wall and found that the

bricks were quite damp and that the white powdery substance was easily brushed off.

(d) A closer examination of the stains showed that they were located directly under the vertical joints in the coping stones and were not easily brushed or scraped off the brickwork.

(e) Finally, they examined the coping and found that the drip stopped short of the ends of each stone. Also it was noted that there was no damp-proof course under the stones.

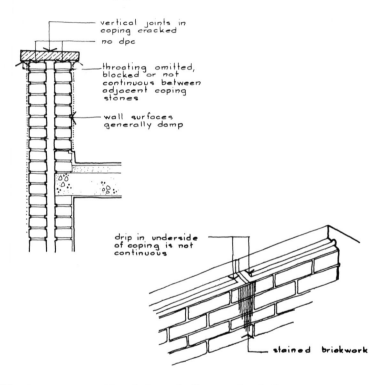

The two men considered these findings and asked:

Q.15. 4 Why were they unable to see the powdery substance on the first visit, and why is the substance more prominent on the outer wall face? What substance would easily brush off the surface?

Q.15. 5 Was there any relationship between the stains and the incomplete drip under the stone?

Q.15. 6   Could the absence of a damp-proof course under the stone be contributing to the stains?

Q.15. 7   What is the staining and white powder?

Conclusions

Both men were agreed that the stains and the white powdery substance were crystallised salts on the surface of the brickwork, commonly known as efflorescence.

Q.15. 8   What type of salts are they, and how could they get on to the brickwork?

Q.15. 9   What measures can be adopted to cure the trouble?

16. The case of the rotating wall

To complete a large housing contract, a builder was asked by the architect to provide half brick walls to screen twenty courtyards between existing buildings from the view of the new estate. Although it was not easy for the builder to get the materials for this additional work, he was finally successful and completed all the work within two weeks of the request.

When measuring the work during the week following completion the quantity surveyor noticed vertical joint cracks in four of the walls which, in each case, was close to the return end of the wall. He decided to raise the matter with the builder before authorising payment of the work.

Verbal Investigation

(a) The quantity surveyor called in at the builder's office and raised the matter with the contracts manager responsible for that job and others in the area.

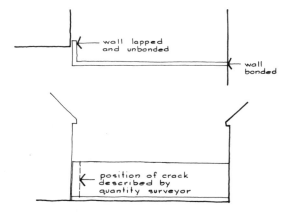

(b) The contracts manager produced a copy of the architect's original drawing for the walls and the surveyor sketched in the position of the cracks.

Q.16. 1 Having told the quantity surveyor that he was not ready to commit himself on the cause at this point and would investigate the matter, the manager considered the information given to him to see if there existed any clues to the nature of the problem. Was any of the information useful? If so, what, and how is it useful?

Site Investigation: first stage

(a) As the Easter holidays occurred just after the quantity surveyor's visit, it was a further ten days before the contracts manager, accompanied by the foreman responsible for the work, visited the site.

(b) On looking at one of the faulty walls, they were alarmed to see that the cracking was far more severe than described. The vertical brick joints close to the corner of the wall on both elevations had opened. Some bricks had also cracked.

(c) They then saw that only the wall above the damp-proof course had cracked and that it was out of alignment with the walling below the damp-proof course.

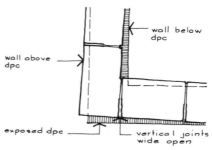

plan showing relative positions of walling above and below the dpc

(d) They next examined both ends of the wall where it met the existing buildings. At the end where the short wall return laps the existing brickwork, it was clearly seen that the wall was rotating about the corner of the building. The other end had been bonded into the existing brickwork, was firm, and had not moved.

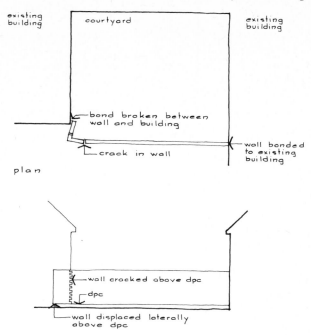

(e) Moving to the other walls which were said to be cracked, they found virtually the same type and degree of failure.

(f) Fearing the worst, they now visited the remaining sixteen walls, and to their relief found they were undamaged.

Before making any further inspections, they went to a neighbouring cafe to have a cup of tea. Over this, they discussed the following questions:

Q.16. 2 What patterns or arrangements of forces on the wall could cause this type of wall movement? Where would these forces come from?

Q.16. 3 Why has the movement only affected the brickwork above the damp-proof course?

Q.16. 4 Why might only four of the twenty walls be affected?

Verbal Investigation: second stage

They both thought the most probable cause of failure was wall expansion and so the contracts manager asked his foreman a number of questions:

73

(a) Were the four defective walls built at a different time from the others?

(b) Did he think the bricks were all right? Was the mortar all right?

(c) What was the weather like when the walls were built?

The foreman, after some thought, said the four walls were the last ones built. He was able to complete all the foundations with the other walls but unfortunately ran out of bricks and had to await a special delivery. The clay bricks were exactly the same as those used in the other walls and for that matter the same type used on the housing contract; he thought it most unlikely that there was something wrong with the brick, and if there was, it was not possible to see the fault.

On the question of the mortar mix, he was once again doubtful whether there was anything wrong because the men who built the walls were engaged on all of them and were very experienced and expert bricklayers.

The weather was described as being very mild with occasional showers of rain which did not significantly prevent working.

Q.16. 5 From this conversation, the manager was able, with confidence, to commence a process of eliminating some possible causes. What causes could he eliminate?

Site Investigation: second stage

(a) To confirm some of the information given by the foreman, they made one more visit to the walls.

(b) Firstly, they examined the mortar joints and found that the material was quite firm and showed no signs of crumbling or general disintegration.

(c) Secondly, they visually compared the brickwork in the four faulty walls with that in the remainder and found no difference. In both cases the bricks looked firm and in good order.

(d) Finally, feeling rather baffled, they looked at the existing buildings to see whether there was any sign of movement that may have affected the wall. There were no signs of such movement.

Q.16. 6 This inspection confirmed in their minds that the fault must be the result of unusual behaviour by the bricks. They asked themselves how the bricks might behave abnormally and what would cause them to do so?

Conclusion

The contracts manager returned to his office and telephoned the supplier, who recalled the special request for a small quantity of bricks to finish the work and said he would look into the matter and come to the site.

When the supplier arrived and had seen the wall, he told the contracts manager that the trouble was due to the design of the wall not being able to accommodate brick expansion which had occurred as the result of newly fired bricks taking in moisture from the atmosphere.

Q.16. 7 How does this expansion process take place?

Q.16. 8 What type of measures are needed to overcome the problem of brick expansion?

Q.16. 9 How else could this wall have been constructed to overcome these problems?

17. The case of the dangerous garden walls

Situation

A group of house owners decided that they would like their back gardens screened properly from a busy main road and so agreed to share the cost of having a wall built. They obtained a number of quotations and finally selected a firm of bricklayers because they submitted the lowest prices and promised to complete the work quickly.

The bricklayers who constructed the wall to their own design and specification completed the work on time and the agreed cost. However, within one year the wall had cracked and bulged in places to such an extent that the local authority decided it constituted a danger to the general public. The local authority shored the wall up while the owners decided whether to pull it down or undertake repairs.

At a meeting the owners decided to consult a professionally qualified surveyor before taking any steps to correct the trouble and nominated one of the group to represent them.

Verbal Investigation

The next day the person elected 'phoned a colleague who was a professional surveyor and related the problem. The surveyor said he would act for them and asked the following questions:

(a) When was the wall built and how old is it?
(b) What are the wall dimensions?
(c) When were the cracks first noticed and where are they located?
(d) How many cracks are there?
(e) Have any other walls in the district failed?
(f) Did any of the house owners have any views on reason for failure?

In reply the house owners said the wall had been constructed in

November which meant that it was eleven months old. There were three or four vertical cracks which had all occurred in the middle section of the wall and they had first been noticed last May. Some of the house owners thought the wall might have been too thin and had buckled during the windy April weather, although no other walls in the district had failed. However, this wall was longer and higher than other neighbouring walls, being approximately 60 metres long and 3 metres high. It was half a brick thick.

Q.17. 1   This information was useful to the surveyor in diagnosing the cause of the trouble. What could he learn from it?

Site Investigation: first stage

On arriving the surveyor viewed the outside of the wall from the street.

(a)   He noticed that the wall dimensions were approximately as described and the wall spanned between existing buildings. The wall was also divided into ten bays with alternate ones set back from the front wall line.

(b)   A closer examination showed that the cracking was very pronounced in the three projecting bays at the middle of the wall. Other bays showed hair line cracking. Some cracking had occurred close to the brick piers dividing the bays.

(c)   Only the wall above the damp proof course had cracked and

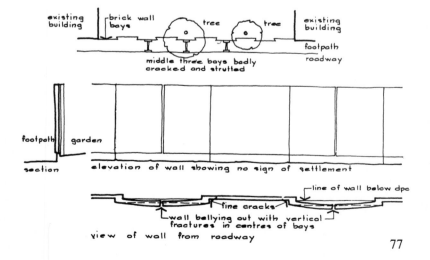

77

The case of the dangerous garden walls

The case of the dangerous garden walls

bowed outwards and there was no sign of any failure whatsoever in the walling below this level.

The surveyor then went into the gardens to inspect the back of the wall.

(d)   The gardens sloped gently down to the wall and finished on average one or two brick courses below the damp proof course.

(e)   A tree was situated just behind one of the wall cracks.

The surveyor now considered the following questions:

Q.17. 2   Why had the cracking only occurred above the damp-proof course?

Q.17. 3   Why are the cracks more pronounced in the centre bays?

Q.17. 4   Why was the cracking mainly restricted to the projecting bays?

Q.17. 5   Would the presence of the tree have caused the failure?

Site Investigation: second stage

The location of the cracks and the bulging outwards had convinced the surveyor that failure had occurred through movement in the length of the wall.

Q.17. 6   What could cause movement along the length?

One answer to the above question could be that one or both of the buildings at either end were exerting pressure on the wall. The surveyor looked at this possibility and found no evidence of any movement in the existing building.

Conclusion

The wall failed because the buildings at either end and the lack of expansion joints prevented normal thermal expansion of the bricks to be accommodated without wall distortion.

Q.17. 7   What was the main evidence which contributed to the conclusion that thermal expansion had occurred?

Q.17. 8   What degree of thermal expansion is likely to take place in brick walls?

Q.17. 9   What remedial measures need to be taken?

18. The case of the twelve similar cracks

Not many months after the completion and occupation of twelve terraced brick houses, one of the owners became quite worried by the appearance of a crack in the brickwork above the back door. His worries were further increased by the fact that cracking was present above the back door in all the other properties. He feared that a major failure was occurring and in talking to all the other house owners he created a general feeling of anxiety amongst them which resulted in the group asking the speculative builder to meet them on site to discuss repairs as a result of the following letter.

Written evidence: first stage
The letter said:

> 10 The Terrace,
> New Village.
> 9th September.

Dear Mr. Mason,

I have been asked by all the owners of the above terrace to write to you and ask for a meeting next Saturday morning at the above address to discuss remedial work to existing cracks in the back walls of all the properties and measures to prevent further failures taking place. Each house has developed a crack in the brickwork which runs from the top of the back door to the underside of an upper window.

It is now approximately five months since we occupied our houses and most of us first noticed the cracks about three months ago and feel that they have got worse.

I have been asked to remind you that the defects maintenance period of six months is still operative and to ask that you give this matter your earliest attention to avoid what could be a most serious building collapse.

> Yours faithfully, A. G. Tate

81

Q.18. 1   This letter was typical in that it was more designed to promote action rather than provide detailed information on the failure. However, it did give the builder some leads as to the cause. What were they?

Examination of Contract Documents

In reply Mr. Mason agreed to meet the owners but refrained from commenting on the damage. He now compiled some of the information he had on the properties, as follows:

(a)   The houses were all completed during March and early April and were progressively handed over to the owners over that period.

(b)   The outer walls were of cavity construction using sand lime facing bricks on the outer skin and lightweight concrete blocks on the inside.

(c)   The lintol over the door in question was formed by using a steel angle under the outer skin and a concrete lintol on the inner skin. Elsewhere all other openings were formed by the use of concrete boot lintols.

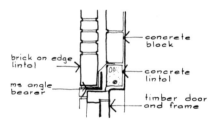

(d)   The brickwork below the d.p.c. was in a different type of sand lime brick.

(e)   The front of the house was faced in lapped boarding.

Q.18. 2   This information refreshed the builder's memory on a number of points and enabled him to identify some special features of construction which may be linked with the failure. What were they?

Site Investigation: first stage

After hearing a number of emotional outbursts from some of the owners the builder was finally able to conduct an inspection of all the properties and as a result was relieved to find that:

(a) the cracks were in all cases hairline;
(b) there was no cracking in other parts of the structure either inside or outside;
(c) the brickwork below the doorstep was not cracked;
(d) the brick wall was in perfect alignment and had not bulged nor had it dropped out of level.

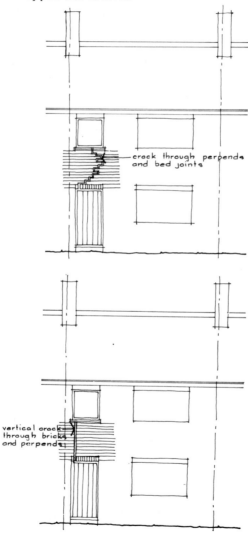

Mr. Mason was now able to answer these important questions which had arisen from the inspection:

Q.18. 3 What type of cracking failure could occur in an outer skin only?

Q.18. 4 What type of failure would leave the brickwork in level and in perfect alignment?

Q.18. 5 Why had the wall cracked in this position?

Conclusion

The builder concluded that drying shrinkage had taken place in the sand-lime bricks which had shown itself in a position of low resistance to horizontal movement.

Q.18. 6 What was the main evidence for these conclusions?

Q.18. 7 How can this form of shrinkage be minimised?

Q.18. 8 What remedial measures can be adopted?

19. The case of the innocent local authority

The owners of an end terraced house noticed some cracks on the external and internal faces of an external wall just above a kitchen window near one corner of their house. At the time of first spotting them, the husband was assured by his wife that they had been there for years, and eventually he filled them with mortar. However, they proceeded to grow and when new ones appeared he began to suspect that a recent road widening job alongside his house was causing the trouble.

Hoping to pin the blame and costs of repairs on to the local authority, the owner consulted a professional surveyor, who, at an interview asked some background questions:

Verbal Investigation
(a) How old is the house?
(b) When were the cracks first noticed?
(c) How long after the first repair did the cracks reappear?
(d) How long after the road construction did the cracks appear?
(e) Where is the road in relation to the building and the cracks?
(f) Could he think of any reason for the failure?

The owner said the house was fifty years old and the cracks were first noticed by him two years ago and six months after the road was completed The road was only 7 metres from the cracked walls. The cracks had reappeared within a month of repairing, i.e. last month.

The only reason for the failure could be vibration from the heavy container lorries that now travelled along the road.

Q.19. 1 These answers got the surveyor thinking about the cause. What thoughts would he be developing?

Further verbal investigation and information search
Having been told that the cracking had followed road widening work

the surveyor called on the local authority to examine the documents for the scheme. From this search he gleaned the following information:

(a) The road was formed of a 150 mm reinforced concrete slab on 300 mm of selected hardcore.

(b) The soil was light clay.

(c) Existing house foundations were surveyed prior to the work commencing and were found to comprise 225 mm solid brick walls resting on a normal 150 mm thick concrete strip foundation located 1066 mm below ground level.

(d) Ground levels were reasonably constant over the whole area.

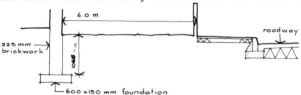

Q.19. 2 This information was particularly useful in helping the surveyor to decide whether the road works had been responsible for the building failure. What conclusions could be drawn from it?

Site Investigation: first stage

(a) The next day the surveyor visited the site and before calling at the house he looked at other houses in the area They were all of a similar design and none of them appeared to be cracked.

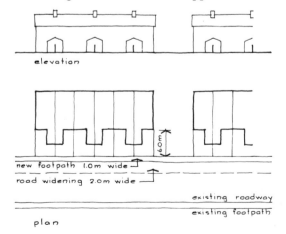

(b) The road had been widened by approximately 2 metres which meant that the footpath was now 6 metres away from the back wall of the terraced houses.

(c) The external walls were built in stock bricks and the type of bonding confirmed the survey drawings which showed the walls to be one brick thick.

(d) On entering the garden the surveyor observed serious cracking in the external walls at one corner. There were numerous cracks whose position indicated that the corner of the building was settling (see Case Study 1).

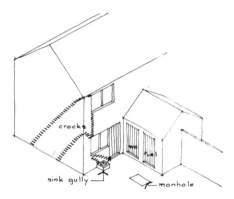

(e) At this point the owner joined the surveyor and asked him if he thought that the building had sunk through vibration and in so doing had broken the drains. In this connection the house owner pointed to the very damp ground adjacent to the cracked walls.

The surveyor told the owner that he would like to have a hole dug alongside the foundations to inspect them before making any comment on the cause and that it would be advisable to conduct a drain test.

All this evidence raised a number of interesting questions:

Q.19. 3 What evidence is there to suggest the wall is settling?

Q.19. 4 Is the question of drain failure relevant to this problem? If so, how?

Site Investigation: second stage

(a) By examining the manhole close to the wall it was found that the connection from the w.c. flowed properly but that no water discharging into the gully was entering the manhole.

Q.19. 5 This led the surveyor to ask: where was the water discharging?

Site Investigation: third stage

(a) The excavations revealed that the back of the gully was cracked and that water had run into the soil, causing it to become soft in an area stretching from the kitchen door to the corner of the building.

(b) The soft soil extended down to a depth of 2 m.

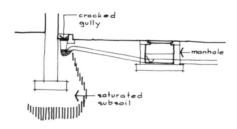

Conclusion

The gully had been cracked for many years before the road was built and water discharging into the ground had progressively weakened the bearing strength of the soil. This weakening had ultimately resulted in foundation settlement and cracking wall. Whether road works and traffic vibration had accelerated the process of failure was in doubt.

Q.19. 6 What were the most important pieces of evidence leading to this conclusion?

Q.19. 7 How could road works and vibration accelerate the failure?

Q.19. 8 What remedial measures are required?

20. The case of the suspect extension

After complaining long and hard about the lack of room in her kitchen, a wife finally provoked her husband into agreeing to removing an outer fuel store and building on a kitchen extension.

A small firm, just formed to specialise in extension work, obtained the contract which included designing and getting approvals for the work. From the married couple's point of view the price was reasonable, the work was done quickly and they got the space and design which enabled the lady to build her dream kitchen.

After three years, damp patches were observed just above skirting level on either side of wall which divided part of the old from the new kitchen accommodation. The couple tried to contact the builders of the extension but found they had long since disbanded and moved out of the district.

The advice of a small builder was sought and he suggested that it might be condensation. As a result, he was given a contract to build a ventilator in a wall to extract moist air from the kitchen. This, alas, did not cure the trouble and with the patches getting larger the couple finally approached a friend who was well qualified in building to examine the dampness.

Verbal Investigation
Over a few drinks in a club, and hearing the above story, the friend asked the couple some questions about the house and the problem.
(a)   Where precisely was the dampness appearing?
(b)   Were any other parts of the kitchen or, for that matter, of the house, similarly affected?
(c)   How old was the house?
(d)   How thick was the wall in question?
(e)   What type of floor did both the old and new sections have?
(f)   Did water lie on the ground outside the extension?

The couple said the house was built in the early 1930's and had solid walls and not cavity ones as is usual today. However, the builders did construct cavity walls in the extension but the damp wall was part of the old external solid wall. To illustrate this the husband drew a sketch.

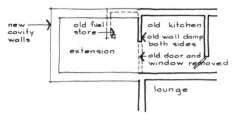

After explaining the drawing the husband said that there was no other signs of dampness and there had never been any in the twenty years they had lived in the house. There was no water lying outside.

The floor in the two sections were different, the part which belonged to the original building being timber boarded on floor joists whereas the floor of the extension was solid concrete on concrete rubble.

Q.20. 1 This conversation helped the friend to build up some theories on the nature of the dampness. What might these ideas be?

Site Investigation: first stage

The friend told the couple that the evidence suggested that dampness appeared to be the result of faulty construction around the original external wall area and made arrangements to visit the house and make an inspection.

(a) On arrival he first inspected the patches and surrounding area and found that the dampness formed an uneven horizontal line a little way above the skirting on either side of the wall.

(b) The solid floor had a thermoplastic floor covering and extended to the inner face of the original external wall.

(c) He then took out the skirting on the dividing wall and some floor boards and noted that the dampness extended down the wall to the damp-proof course and also below that to the over-site concrete.

(d) This underfloor inspection also revealed that the wall plate and floor joists resting on the sleeper walls were quite dry.

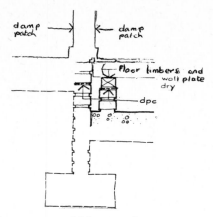

This inspection prompted him to ask:

Q.20. 2 How could the wall become damp above the damp-proof course?

Site Investigation: second stage

The restriction of the dampness to the dividing wall directed the friend towards an inspection of the conditions of the solid floor and underfloor behind the wall.

(a) He removed some brick work just above the damp-proof course which exposed the edge of the floor covering, concrete floor and hardcore.

(b) All the brickwork removed was damp, as was the edge of the floor slab and its supporting brick hardcore.

(c) The only damp proofing in the solid floor was by means of a bitumastic bedding material for the thermoplastic tiles.

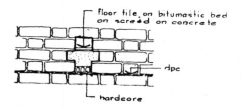

Conclusion

The friend concluded that dampness rising from the ground into the

91

brick hardcore had entered the wall above the damp-proof course
and had thence travelled up the wall.

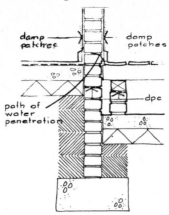

Q.20. 3 What was the main evidence supporting this conclusion?

Q.20. 4 What types of construction could have prevented it
happening?

Q.20. 5 What remedial measures can now be adopted?